GROWING UP IN GUYANA

FORMERLY BRITISH GUIANA

Wipey

GROWING UP IN GUYANA FORMERLY BRITISH GUIANA

iUniverse books may be ordered through booksellers or by contacting:

iUniverse
1663 Liberty Drive
Bloomington, IN 47403
www.iuniverse.com
1-800-Authors (1-800-288-4677)

Because of the dynamic nature of the Internet, any web addresses or links contained in this book may have changed since publication and may no longer be valid. The views expressed in this work are solely those of the author and do not necessarily reflect the views of the publisher, and the publisher hereby disclaims any responsibility for them.

Any people depicted in stock imagery provided by Getty Images are models, and such images are being used for illustrative purposes only. Certain stock imagery © Getty Images.

ISBN: 978-1-5320-4578-3 (sc)
ISBN: 978-1-5320-4579-0 (e)

Library of Congress Control Number: 2018903415

Print information available on the last page.

iUniverse rev. date: 03/28/2018

by Wipey

PREFACE

I decided to write this book because I felt that I needed people to have a better understanding of me and thus a better appreciation for the person that I am today. I felt that I needed to write this book so as to keep a record of my life as I grew up in my beautiful native British Guiana. This book could also be used by my relatives, grandchildren, and friends as a documentary of life in British Guiana then, as seen through my eyes.

ACKNOWLEDGEMENTS

I acknowledge the Lord God who is my savior and without him, I wouldn't be able to do anything. Thank you dear Lord!

I thank my brother/cousin Bernard Blair for supplying me with so many of my pictures and all his worthy advice and assistance. My sister/cousin Golda Blair-Gaskin, was also very helpful and instrumental as she too greatly assisted me. I must also thank Leslyn Wilson-Charles, my sister, who helped to supply me with some pictures and my sister Neibert Wilson who assisted me with some clarifications and explanations.

Mervyn Morris, my son, has been so helpful and patient in assisting me with the very technical aspects of uploading my pictures. Faith Ann Bovell-Patterson has also been very helpful as I kept "bugging her" for names of some of our cousins.

Michelle Porter-Bradshaw has given a lot of information and dates and for all this, I'm so grateful. Last, but not least, I thank all of my relatives and friends for all the encouragement and support they showed me throughout it all. Sometimes, it was just the thought of you that kept me pressing on until I have finally arrived at the very end.

CONTENTS

CHAPTER 1

Land of my Birth

My name is Yvonne Pamela Morris née Wilson. I was born on May 2, 1960 in the beautiful sun filled country of British Guiana in South America to the proud parents of Inez Isabella Roberta Wilson née Blair and the late Leslie Oswald Wilson. I was the third and last daughter born to my parents. My parents and other siblings were at that time living at Cane Grove on the East Coast of Demerara which is approximately 18 miles or 29.968 km from Georgetown, the capital. Our family is of African descent, one of the six (6) ethnic groups residing in Guyana. I was born at the Davis Memorial Hospital which was privately owned and managed by the Seventh Day Adventists. During that time the hospital was located at Barima Avenue, Bel Air Park, Georgetown, Guiana, just about three blocks away from my uncle's and aunt's (Dr. Samuel & Joyce Blair) home. We were not members of the Seventh Day Adventists body, but it was the only privately owned hospital that my family was familiar with and frequented as needed.

To this day, my mom never told me why they ended up calling me by my middle name Pam (Pamela) and not my first. The closest she came to telling me anything concerning my name is that I was not supposed to be named Yvonne, but Yonette and they had forgotten the name by the time I was born. Nevertheless, I grew to love the name Pam and all my relatives knew me by that name. However, when I started school, I had to get accustomed to people calling me by the name Yvonne (this was strange and unusual to me). Now, many of my relatives do not know that my name is also Yvonne, and as the years have gone by, I am usually able to tell which friends I knew from my home environment and those from my school environment. Sometimes this was weird, because on one occasion when a friend came to our home asking for Yvonne, one of my sisters said "There's no Yvonne living here". As soon as she said that, she suddenly remembered and quickly apologized then told the young man to wait a minute as she went to call me. Now isn't that strange or weird to you? See what I'm talking about? That's just what I mean!

Guyana, formerly named British Guiana is a country found in the Caribbean. It is not an island, neither is it in nor near the Caribbean Sea. However, due to its shared history and culture it is considered to be a Caribbean country. Guyana is a founder member of CARICOM (which formerly meant Caribbean Community Market. It now means Caribbean Common Market) which was established in 1973. This country was once ruled by the British, hence its former name British Guiana. As you examine the map of South America, you would notice that Guyana is one of thirteen countries that make up South America and also part of Latin America. Guyana, which is about the size of Idaho, in the United States of America, is about 83, 000 square miles or 214, 970 sq. km and it is the only South American country where English is the official first language. Our neighbor to the east is the Dutch speaking country of Suriname and our western neighbor is Spanish speaking Venezuela. To the south and southwest is Brazil, where their official language is Portuguese. The huge Atlantic Ocean is to the north of our country and as a result of all the damage done whenever there are high-tides, a 'sea-wall' was built along the coast to try to keep the waters out. However, over the years, when the tide comes in, the water just comes in with such great force and speed that it just jumps over the wall as if it's in some high jumping competition.

Guyana's six (6) distinct ethnic groups are East Indians, African descendants, European descendants, Portuguese, Chinese (Asians) and the Amerindians (our indigenous people). However, we do have many mixed groups who reside all over the country. In 2016, the estimated population of Guyana was 769, 722 and most people live along the coastlines. The East Indians consist of about 54% of the population and then the African descendants make up about 44%. For many years there has always been some amount of unrest, rivalry and fighting amongst these two of our largest ethnic groups. This has been going on since way back in the early 50's as I am made aware. Much of it has to do with political power and wealth.

As I was growing up our country was ruled by a Governor General and later a President. Our first Guyanese-born Governor General Sir David Rose was born on April 10, 1923. His father was a proud Georgetown medical doctor and he grew up in Mahaica, East Coast Demerara, about 20 ½ miles or 33 km away from Georgetown.

On May 26, 1966, our country became independent from the British government. We changed the name and spelling to Guyana (meaning land of many waters) and we also got our own flag. Our flag is named the

Golden Arrowhead and it is a rectangular shaped flag that consists of five colors. The flag is green based with a red isosceles triangle (on the hoist side). This is superimposed on a long yellow or gold arrowhead. There is a narrow black border between the red and the yellow and a narrow white border between the yellow and the green. Each color has its significance and the red signifies the zeal of the Guyanese people, while the black shows their strength. The yellow shows the gold and other minerals, while the white represents the waters and river-ways. Lastly but not least is the green that represents the vastly rich forestry that is so underexploited in this country.

Sadly, our Guyanese-born Governor General died in England after being involved in a freak accident on November 10, 1969. As he, his son and other passengers were traveling in a car along a street at Whitehall Place, Westminster, a scaffold fell and crushed the car. He was the only one in the car who was killed, while his son and two other persons were injured. His body was returned to Guyana and he was the first hero to be buried at the Seven Ponds (Place of the Heroes) in the Botanical Gardens in Georgetown, Guyana.

After his death, the David Rose school for mentally challenged students was named in his great honor. Then in the town of Mackenzie Linden, an avenue was also named in his memory. It was believed that when our country had become a republic in 1970, our Governor General was supposed to be named as our first President of Guyana. What a sad loss!

When Guyana became a republic on February 23, 1970, we had our first President and he was sworn into office on March 17, 1970. He was born on January 10, 1918 and grew up in Windsor Forest on the West Bank of Demerara, about 5 miles or 8 km away from Georgetown. He remained our President until October 6, 1980. He died on June 23, 2008 at the long lived age of 90. He was the first ethnic Chinese head of state in a non-Asian country, but his office was really a ceremonial one, since the real power of the country was in the hands of the Prime Minister at that time.

Our first Prime Minister Linden Forbes Sampson Burnham was born on February 20, 1923 in Kitty in British Guiana. He took up this office as Prime Minister from 1964 until 1980 when he became the President of Guyana. When Guyana became a Cooperative Republic in 1970, the President and his government affiliated themselves with communist countries and then nationalized foreign owned bauxite mines and sugar plantations. It is believed that these policies as well as some others led to our economic stagnation in the 80's.

This first executive president of Guyana, led this country for a total of twenty one years before he died on August 6, 1985 at the Public Hospital in Georgetown. I remembered being home on my August vacation

(Summer break as called here in the USA) and listening to the radio station as they played their nice 'catchy up-beat' music. When suddenly the type of music changed drastically and the radio announcers stopped talking or giving any commentary as they usually did. This was occurring on both of our two nationally owned radio stations. Right away I knew something was wrong, but didn't know what it was. This type of solemn music continued for quite a while and immediately I picked up the phone to call somebody to find out what was going on. Of course the phones were busy (at that time we did not have call waiting, just a busy tone), so people started to come out of their houses trying to speak with their neighbors to find out if anybody had heard any news. Of course by now all sorts of rumors started to circulate and one of them was that "fat boy had died on the operating table" (people were referring to the president as 'fat boy' as he was big in statute), as some people knew he was going into the hospital that same day to have surgery done on his throat.

It took the radio stations over an hour before they actually came back on the air to inform the listening public about the President's trip out of the country for emergency surgery. The radio announcers didn't say that the president had died as yet, but that he was gravely ill and had to be flown out of the country. They said that the then Prime Minister had stepped up and taken on the position of the Acting President. Immediately after this announcement, some people started calling the radio stations and asking all sorts of questions. While yet others called in and offered prayers and best wishes to both the President and Acting President.

It was announced a day or two later that on August 6, 1985, our beloved President had died. It is always sad to have to go through the grieving process, but as the saying goes, "live we may, die we must". However, life went on. During the president's era, he had named a housing development Roxanne Burnham Gardens after one of his daughters. A bridge was built across the Demerara River and it was called the Demerara Harbour Bridge or some people used to refer to it as the LFSB – Longest Floating Single Bridge, this is also the initials of the then president. This bridge measures 6, 074 ft. or 1, 851 m in length and connects the people from the East Bank of Demerara to the West Bank of Demerara. At the time when it was constructed in 1978, it was the world's longest toll-paying floating bridge. It was only meant to be a temporary bridge lasting for 10 years, but to date, it still stands there. It seems that there are no plans to make the bridge 4 into a much more secure and permanent structure.

A picture of the Demerara Harbour Bridge

Guyana has many places and streets that have been named after some of our early inhabitants. For instance Vlissengen Road is a Dutch word and so also are fort Kyk-over-al, fort Nassau and fort Zeelandia. Kaieteur Falls is an Amerindian name and it is the name of one of our most beautiful water falls. In fact it has the longest single drop fall in the world measuring 741 ft. or 226 m from the top or plunge area which flows over a series of steep cascades and this added to the first part gives an overall total height of 822 ft. or 251 m. Kaieteur is also one of the most powerful waterfalls in the world with a water flow rate of about 23, 400 cubic ft. per second or 663 cubic m per second.

Picture of Kaieteur Falls

The three largest rivers in the country are the Berbice, Demerara and Essequibo rivers. The country is divided into three counties based on these rivers. The largest river is the Essequibo river measuring 628 miles or 1,010 km in length, next is the Berbice river measuring 370 miles or 595 km and lastly is the Demerara river measuring 215 miles or 346 km. Essequibo is the largest county occupying about 75% of the country, while Berbice is the second largest county and Demerara is the smallest county, but the most important one. Georgetown, the capital of Guyana is located in Demerara. The President's residence, state houses, Parliament Buildings, the St. George's Cathedral (the tallest wooden building in the world) and many countries' embassies are also located in Demerara, hence its great importance. Georgetown is known as the Garden city, because of its lush greenery and all the beautiful green trees surrounding it.

CHAPTER 2

My Early Years: Primary/Elementary School

My father, Leslie Oswald Wilson, became gravely ill sometime in 1960 and subsequently died on January 13, 1961. I was a mere baby only 8 months old, so of course I don't know nor have any recollection of my dad. This really hurts not having my dad around to help raise, nourish, teach, love and spoil me throughout my life. It was during the year 1961, a little after January 13th that my mom, my two older siblings – Leslyn Olivia Wilson-Charles, Neibert Ann Wilson and myself moved into the home of my dear beloved uncle (uncle Sammy, cousin Sammy, Brother Sammy) and aunt (aunty Joyce, cousin Joyce, sister Joyce). My uncle and aunt were living in Bel Air Park, Georgetown, which was an upscale area. My uncle (my mother's younger brother) stepped in and took the place of my dad, so I did have a wonderful male influence in my life. If you had met my uncle, you would understand when I say that he was indeed my father by the way he treated my other siblings and me. Uncle made no distinctions between his own children and us.

My uncle was Dr. Samuel Joseph Blair, an optometrist and optician (I paid tribute to him in my first book My Experiences of a Great Man) who was indeed a man of God and as was said he was the "poor people's eye doctor", as he made his services affordable to all classes of people that he served. Uncle set up 2 out of town part-time offices to help reach other persons in the country. One was in Mackenzie, a town about 67.17 miles or 108 km away from Georgetown, and the other was in New Amsterdam, (a town in Berbice which is approximately 58.62 miles or 94.34 km from Georgetown). He went to the Mackenzie (later renamed Linden) location more often than the Berbice location and it was during some weekends. Sometimes he would use the post office system to return repaired or new glasses to those 2 locations where the patients would go to collect their glasses when they were promised.

A picture of my uncle and my mom maybe in the 1950s.

My aunt was like a second mom to me, because she was always there to help my mom in raising my sisters and me. She was Leslyn's Godmother and really loved by us all. Now, I have said in my first book and I will say it again that my aunt had a huge heart and she was extremely loving to open up her doors to us – my mom, Leslyn 4 years 1 month old, Neibert 2 years 7 months old and myself. My uncle and aunt were already raising their family, which consisted of Peter Alexander 3 years old and Joseph Anthony (lovingly called Joey by us) 2 weeks old . My aunt not only welcomed us in, but she allowed us to live there with them for ten long years. During that time, Robert Andrew was born and then later Bernard Anson. As we lived together and our lives got closer, we even began to share our families and relatives. For instance, we (all seven children) acted as if all of the Frasier-Blair's' relatives were also the Wilsons' relatives and vice versa. My aunt's maiden name was Frasier. So, we were claiming and calling these relatives cousins, uncles and aunties, when in fact, we were not related at all. However, we all acted and grew up with everybody in this loving environment and no one looking in from the outside could or would ever say that we weren't related.

My sisters and I never called our uncle, "Uncle Sammy", nor our aunt, "Aunty Joyce", we just said uncle and aunty. Our cousins (whom we felt were like our brothers) never called our mom, "Aunty Inez", they just said aunty, just as we did for their mom. This was puzzling and complicated to people when they heard us both (our cousins/brothers and us) talk about "aunty" and it was 2 different persons. Of course when my cousins/brothers spoke about aunty they meant my mom, who was also known as Aunty Inez, Cousin Inez or Sister Inez. On the other hand, when my sisters and I spoke about aunty, we meant Aunty Joyce, Cousin Joyce or Sister Joyce.

During my early years, we all played together, went to school together, went out shopping, or window shopping and even to the movies together. On a few evenings, mostly on the weekends, we (the children) would get dressed with our sleeping clothes or pajamas, then get into the big car (the Ford Zephyer - my uncle's) and the adults – uncle,

Neibert, Leslyn, and me at the centre posing

aunty and mom (mummy, as we called our mothers back home), would be dressed with their regular outdoor clothing and boarded the car too. We would go to the drive-in cinema or theatre which was located on the East Coast of Demerara in a village called Montrose. This village is about 6.8 miles or 11 km from Georgetown. Most times when we went to the drive-in theatre, it would be for a car load show. The reason for wearing our sleeping clothes was that on our way back home, we would fall asleep, so when we returned, it was less work for our preparation for bed.

It was truly amazing and interesting to look back at those years gone by and wonder and imagine how so many of us used to fit into both my aunt's and uncle's cars. We did not have the law about wearing seat belts and who should sit in front or the back of the car, but my aunt and uncle made that decision based on their judgments, if not whom got in the car first. My aunt usually drove a smaller car so in the front seat next to her would be two passengers in that single passenger front seat, while in the back the first person would sit forward, then the next would sit back and that order was alternated until we got to the last person and the end of the car. In my uncle's much larger car, it would be himself and two other passengers on his single long front seat, while in the back, we did the same thing like we did with my aunt's car. But most obviously, more people fitted into my uncle's car as it was much bigger.

My mother never had that thought or urge to want to drive and she was never interested in learning. I believe that she felt that since her husband had died, she did not see how she would be able to afford a car. I can remember this as if it were yesterday when one summer break, my aunt and uncle were out of the country on vacation and one of my sisters had a fall which resulted in a cut on her forehead. My mom needed to take my sister to the hospital and both of the two cars were in the yard, but remember, mom didn't know how to drive, so, she had to ask a neighbor from the next street to please take them to the hospital. He felt it was so ironic that there were cars there, but no driver.

We went to church regularly, but to different churches, since my uncle was following the Catholic faith, while my mom was following the Anglican faith. At one point in my uncle's and mom's life they grew apart (were raised by different family members in different parts of the country) from each other, so the persons whom my uncle was living with took him to the Catholic Church and thus he became a Catholic.

My aunt was a primary school teacher (Elementary) at a public school and she took us all to the same school where she worked, Dolphin Government Primary school, formerly called Broad Street School. We all enjoyed going to this beautiful two-leveled L shaped school although we were not offered any special privileges for being the teacher's children and nieces. In fact, we had to work just as hard as everyone else, if not harder since greater things were expected from a teacher's child.

In the meantime, my mom had taken up a position as a beautician, since she was a former home maker (she loved to sew and make new clothes for us) and now had to work to support us. Over the years, my mom eventually went into the teaching profession. Before my dad's sickness and ultimate death, he was a highly educated teacher on his way to being promoted to a headmaster, or principal. So, it was interesting to see my mom following along in his profession. It was very good for our family to now have two teachers in the home, because when we were on our August (Summer) vacation, we didn't have to have someone else watch us. When my mom wanted to go on vacations, uncle and aunty were the adults who were in charge of us. Also, when my uncle and aunt wanted to go on vacations, my mom was the adult who was home with us. Also, this I believe was a very good arrangement for all concerned. However, I can remember one time that our aunt was in charge of us during a summer break and she had to comb and braid our hair. Remember, she only had boys and was not in the habit of combing any girls' hair, so when she did our braids they were not as tight as when our mom usually did them.

We enjoyed our childhood years tremendously, running, jumping, skipping, hopping and doing everything else that children do. During all of our school breaks, we didn't have to go out of our yard to find children to play with (although we did, who wants to stay home all the time?), because there were seven children living there. Our yard was big and fenced in. It was the Guyanese custom to build a fence around their property, so everybody could take care of their own. Other children were always coming over to our yard to play with whomever they could find.

We had three school terms or semesters during the school year, so we had three breaks that we looked forward to yearly. The Christmas term was our first term of the school year and that began during the first week of September. After thirteen or fourteen weeks of schooling and hard work, we came to the end of that term and looked forward to our three weeks Christmas break.

Our Christmas breaks were nice, bustling and busy, but we definitely looked forward to that time. We celebrated the birth of Jesus Christ by going to church and honoring that sacred time. We also exchanged gifts on December 25th Christmas Day and before that day we prepared special foods to eat on that day and during the season. To us the season was from mid or later December up to January 6th. Some of the foods that we prepared and ate during the Christmas Season were baked chicken with stuffing, roast pork, baked ham, cook-up rice (it is a meal cooked with rice, peas, different types of meat such as beef, pork, salt beef, pig trotters and cow heel, and also the special ingredient coconut milk), pepper pot (a blackish stew prepared with casareep – which is made from the vegetable cassava), and other meats and a large big red hot pepper- hence its name pepper pot), home-made bread, vegetables, black cake (made with fruits and rum), sponge cake (maybe with some fruits), pickled onions and garlic pork. Some of the beverages we consumed were ginger beer, sorrel, mauby and different types of wines including home-made wines. All of these beverages were prepared in the homes and as we were growing up, we loved the aroma that we got every time we passed by the kitchen or any open door or window in the kitchen. The foods too had a particular smell about them that caused you to want to go and sample them before they were even fully prepared. The entire season was a joyous occasion as we spent time with family and friends, and looked forward to the Christmas gifts that we received.

This is a picture taken around Christmas time. We are standing from left to right, Leslyn, Peter, Neibert and me. Ironically, we were standing chronically. Joey is in front on his bike.

As a child growing up, we looked forward to the last day in the year. We called it Old Year's day, then Old Year's night as opposed to some other countries calling it New Year's Eve. I believe it had both similar meanings to whichever country you were in and celebrated it. It was a big thing for us, because it's not every day an old year ends and a new one begins. We were always excited for this day (it was Joey's birthday), as we looked forward to going to church or at least not going to bed so that the new year (midnight) would come and not find you sleeping.

At the stroke of midnight our GDF, Guyana Defense Force would perform a fireworks display in Georgetown, or sometimes we ourselves went outdoors and created our own fireworks by using some home-made materials. An Old Year's Day tradition that we have had passed down from generation to generation is to cook a large pot of cook-up-rice. This was cooked during the late afternoon or early evening before we went to church for the midnight service. When we returned home from church, we would all get a small bowl or plate with the cook-up-rice and eat it. The myth was that we were eating peas first thing in the morning of a new year for prosperity and a long healthy and wealthy life.

I can't really remember when this started, but I had trouble with both my knees whilst I was growing up. Whenever I knelt down, my knees would pain me so very much. I remember my mom taking me to a very prominent doctor (he was not a specialist) in Georgetown to try to determine what was wrong. But, however, he was not able to diagnose my problem. I even remember, that at one time I had started to visit this doctor every month (by now my mom used to send me by myself), but all the different things he kept doing he still couldn't figure out what was wrong and therefore how to relief me of my pains. I used to look at him open his very large doctor's reference book and try to find a diagnosis, but to no avail. As time went by my problem knees would hamper some of my playtime and I tried to ignore it especially when I was running and playing and truly having a great old time.

Many times we played team sports and games with our friends and we always had fun jumping over our neighbors' fences and running down the streets (these were all cul-de-sacs). I remember one of the boys favorite game was "police and thief". They enjoyed it most when the girls had to run behind them and try to catch them. Sometimes when we grabbed onto their shirts, they quickly unbuttoned their shirts whilst still running and let it go, so they got away and we had to continue running to catch them again. We played so many different types of games when we were young and at times I wondered where they originated.

As I look back at those days I wondered where we got that game "Chinese skipping". This was such a dangerous game, but at that time, we never knew or thought about the danger. This game was played with cut-up inner tubes (from bicycles, motor bikes or motor cars) that we tied together at the two ends. Then two persons would stand at the two ends (on the inside of the rope) and hold the rope first at their ankles, while another person would jump in, jump out (straddle the ropes)and even jump on the rope. If they were successful then the rope was taken up to the knees and the same routine was repeated. Once again, the rope was taken up to the waist, then under the arms, then finally to the neck with the same routine being repeated. It was really fun in those days and we totally understood the meaning of the words "childhood days".

We had some other relatives who were also related to us from our maternal grandmother. They were the Porters and the mother's name was Pansy Benn-Porter. Pansy's mother, Evelyn Elvis was the sister of my grandmother, Valerie (pronounced Va-lay-ree) Blair, and there was another sister named Ruth Bowen. I was not privileged to meet my grandmother, because she had passed long before when my mom was in her teen years, but my two great aunts were still alive. We referred to our cousin as Sister Pansy as both she and my mom called each other Sis. Pansy and/or Sis. Inez. When I first knew about the Porters, they were living in Wismar. To get to Wismar, you had to first travel approximately 67.17 miles or 108 km along the Demerara river from Georgetown to Mackenzie, then join a smaller ferry at Mackenzie to cross over the west bank of the Demerara river to Wismar.

On numerous occasions during the August break, our mom took my sisters and me to Wismar to visit with the Porter family. I really did enjoy those times when we ran and played outdoors in the sand with our cousins, Petal, born in 1962 (now deceased), Maurice (lovingly called Buddy), born in 1964, Michelle Porter-Bradshaw born in 1965, Dr. Lowell (Johnny), born in 1966 and Rev. Dr. Rodwell (Alphonso), born in 1967. Sometimes we played outside for almost the entire day and later we would say that we had a "belly full of play". I looked at those trips as little outings and always wonderful times to spend in a different location with family.

While we were at Wismar one holiday, my sisters, Leslyn and Neibert had got lost after they had set out for a walk. So, when they were eventually home and relaying their story to the adults in the home and saying that they were lost, I apparently chimed in and said "me too". That must have been very funny, because it seems that I was not out of the house with them.

In January of 1970, the Porter family moved to Kara Kara in Linden and by then they had a total of 6 children, 4 boys and 2 girls. Rondell (Avis), born in 1968 was added to the earlier born children. During the school breaks, we again went to visit them. By then the Linden-Soesdyke Highway had been built (officially opened in 1969) and it was the first road I can remember travelling on where we had to pay a toll. Before the Porters moved from Linden to Robb Street in Georgetown, 2 more children were born. They were Della born in 1974 and Jan born in 1975. By this time we were growing older and were able to go and visit the Porters in Robb Street, Georgetown whenever we decided to, but we just had to let our mom know where we were. However, as the Porters family increased in size, they needed a larger place to live. So, in 1977, they moved to the house that they still occupy in Laluni Street in Queenstown, Georgetown. The last of the Porter children Dr. Winslade (lovingly called Mikey) was born in 1978.

I can also remember (I'm not very sure of the year, and it might have been sometime in 1969 before the Linden-Soesdyke highway was completed and officially opened.) when our household went on a road trip to Linden. I would have been about 9 years old and I can remember the car getting stuck along the highway on more than one occasions. This was because some parts of the road didn't have asphalt and tar, but sand and the car not having the appropriate tires, kept getting stuck. So, whenever this happened, we had to get out of the car and push it. It was fun to us. However, I can't remember the trip back home, so I want to believe that it was uneventful otherwise I might have remembered something.

As I remember, growing up and playing in the sunshine was very healthy for us, as we were getting lots of vitamin D as well as exercise. We honestly enjoyed all of the time we spent together. The warm climate was always so refreshing and stimulating and at times the heat really did get too hot for us. I remember a very memorable event that took place one day. As I think back, I can only say that we were just acting like the children we were. My aunt had purchased a box of crackers, like she always did. The thing that she did differently was that she did not take it upstairs to the upper level of the house and put it away immediately as she would normally do. She left it on the platform (that is in the middle of the upper and the lower staircase in the house) and maybe said to herself that she would take it upstairs later. However, one of the seven of us obviously opened the box and took a handful of the crackers on his or her way upstairs. Another one of us on the way upstairs also took a handful of crackers as he or she went upstairs. This pattern continued as we all went both up and down the stairs. Can you imagine, all seven children on their way up and down the stairs filling their hands and "stuffing their faces"?

What a shock my aunt received when she went to pick up the box much later in the day and found it so light. As I look back now, I guess she could have got a heart attack, because she never ever expected that. She called my mom to pick up the box and then they opened it to find just a few pieces of crackers at the bottom, that none of us wanted to finish. She was so surprised that she shouted out "look at what these children have done could you believe it"? She was actually blaming her boys alone, but my mom said no, her girls also had a part in this. They verbally scolded us and we really felt bad to know that in one day, we had actually eaten out an entire box that usually lasted us about two or three weeks. Of course that evening we didn't need dinner as we had eaten so much, or maybe we were too ashamed to go have dinner that evening.

When we all went out, yes, all ten of us, (our family) three adults and seven children, it drew a bit of attention and sometimes people would stare at us and maybe wonder whether we all were siblings. Of course when people asked, my uncle always said that they were all his children. My uncle and aunt always treated my siblings and me as if we were indeed theirs. And my mom made no distinction amongst the children either. What was of interest to note was that my mom had three girls, whilst my uncle and aunt had four boys, and because we were so close and united as brothers and sisters together we did get into mischief or trouble. We never had any sibling rivalry as far as I can remember and that must have been because we were all treated the same and shared everything evenly. However, as we were growing and getting older, my mom wanted us (her daughters) to do more housework because we were girls and in those days that was one of the chores that girls were expected to do.

During the work week there were two ladies who came in to help with the housework. One did the cleaning up of the entire house which consisted of two levels and the other did the cooking of the meals for breakfast and lunch. They shared the laundry work between themselves. Our room was off limits for the cleaning, so mom made my sisters and I do the cleaning in our room and our own laundry. For dinner, my aunt or my mom usually prepared it, but as we were getting older, my mom told us (my sisters and me) to get more involved in preparing the dinner and then doing the dishes afterwards.

Sometime during the year 1969, our family (everybody in the household) had returned from an outing. I cannot recollect the occasion, however, we had gone out in the Ford Zephyer (the big car) and upon our return everybody had already left the car, but me. It was still bright in the afternoon and we would usually leave the car windows open. Now, for whatever reason, as I was leaving the car through the left rear door, I decided to push down the pip (the knob on the top of the door near the window) to lock the door. So, once I was out, I closed the door behind me. Unfortunately for me, my left index finger was caught in the doorway. Of course, I quickly tried to pull on the door handle, hoping to get the door open. This didn't work so I started to scream as the pain was so severe. My mom quickly ran out as she heard my loud screams and she too tried pulling on the door handle. But of course to no avail.

I had no idea for how long it was since I had accidentally closed the door on my finger. However, my uncle ran outside and he quickly pulled up the pip, then opened the door. Oh, what a relief! But my finger was almost flat and it looked black and blue. My mom told me to run some tap water over it, so it could cool and thus ease the pain. After running the water over it for a while, mom applied some ice to my finger. The pain finally eased until it stopped.

Over the next few days, my finger was very sore and I noticed the finger nail slowly coming off. As time went by, I could see the new nail emerging from underneath the old one. As the new nail was growing out, I noticed a line running along the length of the nail down the middle, from the base to its tip. The line began at about approximately a little past half the middle of the base line and as it progressed to the tip, the line shifted a little over to the right side of the finger. So, at the tip, the line had reached the middle of the finger nail.

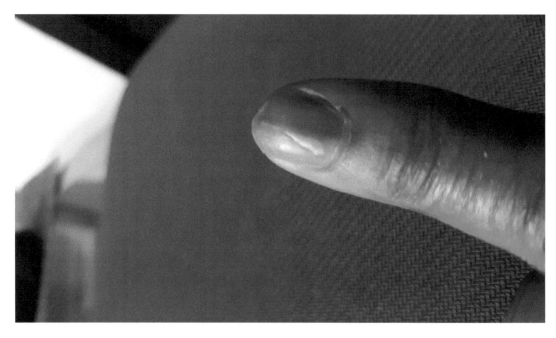

A picture of that left index finger

I didn't understand why there was a line as I thought the new nail could not possibly be affected by that squeeze. Nevertheless, as subsequent nails kept growing out they all came out the same way. As I looked at my finger, it looked like a new nail was coming out from underneath and the old nail was going away, but it seemed like they got caught half way and they both decided to stay. From then on it didn't matter how I cut that nail, it always grew back with that line running down the middle. I guess it is just to remind me of that day when I was not very careful with my finger and the car door. Now when people look at my finger and ask about it (as they often do) I always tell them my story and let them know that they really need to be so careful with their finger and not have to go through my hurting experience.

As mentioned earlier, my dad had died early and so too did most of his siblings. I did not get the chance to meet them with the exception of one, my Aunt Beryl. Aunty Beryl, as we called her, was my father's younger sister, and she was a very short and slim person who was a "busy-body" and a great historian, in her own way. She was very nice and friendly, but if you upset her, you would hear the length of her tongue. I can remember her visiting us in Bel Air Park where we were living and later as I grew older, she had introduced us to some other family members. It was nice to learn about and to actually meet other relatives of my father. Aunty Beryl was a part of my life as far back as I can remember. She attended quite a few functions with us too.

CHAPTER 3

My Middle Years: Secondary/High School Forms 1 - 5

At the end of primary four (grade five), we had to participate in a school leaving examination called Common Entrance. All students 10 years and older had to take this exam in order to gain a place in the Secondary or High School (Middle and High School). If a person was not successful at the first attempt, then they had another chance to repeat the class only if they were not yet 12 years of age. This was a standard exam that was written over a period of two days throughout the country and it tested our mathematics skills, verbal reasoning, reading and comprehension ability as well as our thinking skills. Once this was completed, we moved onto the next stage of our school life. When I took my common entrance, SSEE – Secondary School Entrance Examination, I was awarded Charlestown Government Secondary School. Some of our Secondary schools were Junior High schools while the others were Senior High Schools. Charlestown was a junior high school and we attended it for 5 years, whilst the Senior high schools, students could attend them for either 5 or 7 years.

Our August holidays were always wonderful and every year I looked forward to them, as our friends would continue to come on over, and we continued to have so much fun. One of the many boys who came around to our house was Vibart Yaw, now Dr. Vibart Yaw (dentist and maxillofacial surgeon). His excuse was that he was looking for our mutual friend, Nate, but I believe he was secretly looking for me (smile). I believe that he would leave his house on DaSilva Street, Newtown and stop by our house first, because he had to pass our street, before arriving at Nate's house in the next street. Of course Vibart and I began talking as we were both the same age. I knew from since around then that I liked talking to him and he always wore that wide smile showing his slightly chipped front tooth. I believe that's what attracted the girls (smile), along with his height. Come on now, lots of us girls dreamed of a tall, dark and handsome young man and he was and still is all that.

On one occasion during the August break (summer vacation), as I was visiting my doctor for my aching knees, he flipped through the pages of his very large book again, and said to me that he didn't know what else to do but maybe he could break both legs then open them up to see what was going on inside of them. I said ok (meaning to give myself some-time to think about it as well as to inform my mom) and then left. Now I believe I was in my teen years and the doctor had suggested that we perform this operation during our August vacation. Now this is our long two months break when we get to run, jump, hop, skip, eat lots of fruits and snacks and have a lot of fun being out of school. I was going to be using crutches during that break and merely looking at my siblings, cousins and friends having fun. Oh no! That was not going to happen. That was the very last time that I went to that doctor. I'm sure you would have done the same thing too.

As time went by, my ailment was still a bother to me and sometimes it would pain me without me even having to kneel. So, I learned how to cope with that by not putting my full weight down whenever I had to kneel. You could tell the cartilage in my knees were either worn or not present at all, because whenever I bent them, you could hear the crunching sounds that they made as if bone was rubbing against bone. I can remember once taking advantage of my condition for my benefit, or so I believe. My mom had returned home early from her studies one evening and found me in bed fast asleep, much earlier than my regular bedtime. Immediately, she said that somebody had done me something, so she woke me up and asked what had happened. I complained that my older sister had hit me right around my knee and it hurt so bad that I went in the bed crying until I fell asleep. My mom got very upset by this and scolded her because she knew that I had problems with my knees. It felt good to hear my mom scolding her, as I couldn't and I didn't want to do what Leslyn had told me to.

During one of our August holiday breaks, Vibart had come over looking for Nate, but I had not seen him for the day, so we talked for a long time. Then up came my neighbor Larry who definitely had a huge crush on me. He saw Vibart and me in deep conversation and just kept standing at the gate with a book in his hand. When we were finally finished with our conversation, Vibart left and Larry came in the yard and stood right next to me. He was visually very upset and right away asked me if I didn't see him at the gate waiting for me. Of course I did see him, both Vibart and myself saw him as clear as day and that is why we had cut short our conversation. He said that I was "gaffing and smiling up" (talking and flirting) with Vibart while he was waiting patiently on his girlfriend, me. Nobody had given me that information. Yes, Larry and I were friends and he lived just two yards away from me right there in Barima Avenue, so once he was in the yard or at his windows, he could see anybody or everybody who came to our house. Now Larry actually lived in the United States of America, but during the August holidays, he returned to Guyana to spend his vacation. Of course I felt a bit special now that Larry had called me his 'girlfriend', but we had had no previous discussion about this matter. I knew that Larry was jealous and I don't remember Vibart saying anything about girlfriend, after all I was a girl and also his friend (smile).

Larry was so upset that he didn't even exchange his book, he just left it and hurried back home. For the rest of his vacation, Larry did not come back over to talk to me (he is the one who usually came over). I only saw him when he came over to tell me he was leaving the following day to return to the U.S.A. After that, I have never seen nor do I know what has happened to Larry.

In September of 1971 my uncle's and aunt's family increased even further by the birth of Golda Ann Blair-Gaskin, a beautiful baby girl -the first girl for this wonderful couple. So now my mom knew that we needed to move because of so many reasons. One is that we were growing older and had been living under the Blairs' roof for ten long years now. They needed the room for the baby and the time was just about right now for us to move as we (my siblings and I) were all now attending secondary school. My mom knew that her brother and his wife had helped her a great deal and she was now able to gather her three daughters and together move on to the next stage of our lives. My mom and my uncle were extremely close, just like 'batty and posey' (as referenced in my first book), so for her to move on was not an easy thing to do. However, she plucked up enough courage to inform uncle and aunty of her plans for us to move on.

Here is the house in Bel Air Park, where I grew up with my family.

A picture of Andrea and myself at my home in Norton Street

We were moving to Norton Street, Wortmanville in Georgetown a house my mom had purchased some time ago after my dad had passed. This house was approximately 1 ½ miles away from where we were living in Bel Air Park, Georgetown. However, every weekend my mom, my sisters and I would travel to Bel Air Park just to spend some more time with our family. We loved being together, so the more we were apart, is the more we missed each other.

I had a wonderful stay at Charlestown and met many students with whom I have formed a life-long bond. Many times I have looked back at those very early secondary years and felt as if it were only just the other day, but in reality it was decades ago. One thing I definitely remembered when I had just started Charlestown, was the students trying to make fun of me and calling me an "English duck". Their reason was because I was speaking perfect English (which is what I was accustomed to all my life) and not creolese like so many of them. In our house we were not allowed to speak creolese or broken English. Then when I started to perform well in Spanish class, I was again nicknamed, only this time, "the Spanish duck". In Guyana, it was always so easy for students to make fun of others and give them nicknames or false names as we called it, but these names mainly stuck when the persons kept answering to them. At that early age I didn't realize that this was a form of peer pressure. Some of the many friends that I have met and still correspond with are Andrea Stephens-Farley,

Roxanne Warren, Lawrence Fanfair, Jennifer and Faye Caleb and June Ann Marcus-Thornhill.

It was while I was still attending Charlestown that I became aware that June-Ann Marcus was my cousin. One day her mother, my mother and I met in a street in downtown Georgetown and Cousin Joyce, June-Ann's mom, said her daughter was attending Charlestown too. So, the next day we both went to school, each armed with a name and determined to discover whom this relative was. So we found each other and were pleasantly surprised that we had known each other, but not that we were related. It was even good to now know another member of my father's relatives. Since that day, we have let people know that we are related and you better not mess with any one of us or else you have to deal with both of us.

I remember one day whilst I was in my classroom, one of my male friends started to tease and tantalize (tease or make fun of) me about an older boy in the school. At first, I told him to stop it, but he continued. I repeatedly told him to stop it as it wasn't true, but he again ignored me and got even louder. He got me so angry, that I let fly an object that I had in my hand aiming straight for his head. He had very good reflexes and ducked just in time. That object hit the chalkboard "BANG!" and immediately after straightening up, he told me that he was 'done tantalizing me', because he now realized just how serious I was. True to his word, my

A picture of June-Ann Marcus-Thornhill

21

friend has never ever teased me again and I believe that it was then that he respected me as he found out that I didn't play when it came to certain things. During my life at Charlestown, there were some very attentive and caring teachers that I still wonder what has happened to them over the years.

It is amazing that when you are growing up there are so many things that you pay attention to and find so funny and interesting. At Charlestown, there were two teachers who were always together and deep in conversations, whether they were in the teachers' lounge, on the playground, standing for assembly, just anytime, once they were not teaching. They were quite a funny sight once you saw them together and there wasn't anything wrong with them. However, most of the talking seemed to be coming from just one of the two parties. In fact, it seemed that this teacher was always talking, maybe he had a lot to say, but the other teacher didn't seem to mind. The students referred to the two teachers as "Mutt and Jeff". I guess you figured it out by now, yes, one of the teachers was short and the other was very tall, they were as it looked - at two extremes. The tall teacher was over 7 ft. tall and he was the Physical Education (P.E.) teacher, while the short teacher was just under 5 ft. tall and he was the History teacher, the one who was mainly talking (maybe he was just sharing some of his history). We have a saying that states short people do a lot of talking to make up for the lack of height. Maybe that was true, and also, since History was such a huge topic, he might have always had a lot to talk about. Nevertheless, these teachers seemed to have a bond. The P.E. teacher who was a foreigner to our country and school had introduced our students to many of the other sports and games that were played abroad and very soon a great interest was developed among us. He was also able to set up different teams who eagerly showed their competitiveness and willingness to play.

It was at this stage in my secondary school life that I got involved in sports and athletics and enjoyed every moment of it. Yes, I was a very competitive young lady and didn't like to lose, but I accepted losing gracefully. It was during this time of playing sports that I met many other friends from other schools and organizations. For example, I met Owen Wilkinson, who attended Saints Stanislaus College (one of our senior all males boys' high school). He was a fabulous table tennis player, and I had met him and many others after I had attended a tennis club, called Malteenoes. Oh, he was so fine, and of course tall and good looking, just what we girls liked in a friend or a boyfriend. Mmhh! We became good friends since way back then, and sometimes we would see him and his other friends practicing at the Sports complex, whenever my friends and I attended a work-out session there. Some of those friends I am still in contact with, while I have lost contact with many others.

I had gained an interest in games like basketball, volleyball, lawn tennis (as we called it back home) table tennis and badminton, all because of the exposure that our P.E. teacher had given us. I also discovered that I too had that athletic ability like my mom and older siblings. So every year, I participated in my school's track and field events taking part in the 100, 200 and 400 meters races as well as the 4 x 100 meters relay, high jump and long jump (broad jump) events. I surely enjoyed and miss all these activities now. My house leader was the teacher who mostly encouraged and supported me with my athletics. Incidentally, this was the teacher who was the "talker" mentioned previously. He ensured he held frequent meetings with us and he would even come to our practice field to give further support. Earlier I had found out that this teacher knew my mother and Leslyn, my older sister, because she had previously attended Charlestown for a brief period and he was her history teacher. Before completing my secondary education at Charlestown, my sister Neibert and I joined Ravens, a former male only basketball team where we played a few competitive games. It was great getting to meet and play mixed games against some other teams. We supported our men's team every time they played and they did likewise with us.

A family picture of the Blairs

From left to right: (standing) Peter, aunty, uncle and Joey, (sitting) Robert, Golda and Bernard

At one of my uncle's and aunt's wedding anniversary
From left to right: Bernard, Peter, Robert, aunty, uncle, Golda and my mom in front

CHAPTER 4

My Post High School Years

After completing my secondary education at Charlestown Government Secondary school, I attended a Secretarial Institution to further my studies in short hand, typewriting and book-keeping and I also attended a mathematics class. I was now attending the math class, because whilst in school as I was promoted from form to form or grade to grade, the teachers would change and the type of math would also change from modern math to traditional math, then back to modern math again, then traditional math once more. This was confusing for me as math was not one of my best subjects and I was struggling to keep abreast with the class. So, I had dropped Math. I enjoyed attending these classes now as I was exposed to some new things that I had not learnt before and I was also having fun as I learned.

Also during this time, I was involved in many activities within my church's youth organization. We regularly attended St. Barnabas Anglican church on Regent Street in Georgetown. There were quite a few young people in our church, so we came together and formed a church young people group. It was very interesting and good for us as it was a way of trying to keep us engaged and on the right path. We held most of our activities on Saturday mornings and some meetings were held during the week in the afternoons. It was important for us to belong to that group because youths were an important and integral part of society. We needed to be prepared for the world of work and for life outside of and after school.

During this time, I became a bit more aware of some other maternal relatives. My 2 great-aunts as mentioned previously both had children and grandchildren. Some of them we met earlier in life and some others we just met them later. Evelyn (aunty Evelyn) Elvis had 2 children Michael (Bro. Mike) Elvis and Pansy (Sis. Pansy) Benn-Porter as mentioned earlier. The reason these cousins referred to each other as Sis. and Bro. was because that was their way of showing some respect to their older cousins and not calling them "full mouth" . However, these same older cousins also called their younger cousins Bro. and Sis. and when we, their children came along that's what we called these older cousins. Now, Bro. Mike and his family had migrated to England many years ago, so we weren't too familiar with his 2 children Carol and Colin. Then subsequently he had a new family and 2 more children named Jasmin and Ashton.

On the other hand, Ruth (aunt mother) Bowen also had 2 children. Their names were Clinton Edward (Cousin Bonnie) Bowen and Fay (Sis. Fay) Bowen. Sis. Fay had 3 children, Colin, Donna and Faith-Ann, while Cousin Bonnie had 5 children named Denise (now deceased), Andrew, Mark, Roger, and Penelope (Penny). We were not too close with these relatives but we met them more than once and knew that we were related. Our great aunt was called aunt mother, because my mom and uncle called her 'mother' when she was left in charge of them while their mom worked in Georgetown for the European (white) people. Their mother kept asking them how can your aunt be your mom, when she was your aunt. So, she had to keep telling them that Ruth was their aunt. So, that's how they decided to call her "aunt mother". So, most naturally when we came along we used the same name to address her.

Some other relatives we grew up spending some time with were Frankie (Bro. Frankie) Knights and his family, Doreen (Sis. Doreen) Branche and her son Ricky, Norma (Sis. Baby) Branche and her 2 children Aubrey and Cindy.

I can also remember the times when my mom took us up to Victoria, approximately 16.58 miles or 26.68 km from Georgetown, This was the first village purchased by freed slaves in 1838. My mom's great aunt, Christina (aunt Chris) lived in Victoria and we went to spend some time with her during our Easter and August breaks. Aunt Chris lived near the seawall, so many times we would walk along the seawall and even go out into the Atlantic Ocean. We didn't go out very far into the water, because at that time none of us knew how to swim, but we always enjoyed ourselves wadding around in the water and playing with the sand.

CHAPTER 5

Working with uncle 1977 - 1979

After I had completed these studies and had passed my exams, my mom suggested that I go to "help out" my uncle at his office. Hence began my working days with my uncle in his practice of Optometry. His practice was located in Alexander Street, Lacytown, Georgetown at that time and there I worked along with his wonderful receptionist. Now she had been working along with Dr. Blair for quite some time now before I joined her. During her work life there, apart from being the receptionist, Dr. Blair had taught her some of the technical aspects of the job. Some of these tasks, she in turn taught me after I had been there for some time too.

Later Dr. Blair showed me some of the other technical aspects of the job as he was performing them. One thing I remembered him saying to me is that his job was a hard job to do and as I worked there with him over the years I grew to find out exactly what he was talking about. Before working with my uncle, I didn't know him in terms of his professional side, but it was no different from what I had known before of him. He had taught us so much about how to live our lives and to always strive for our own success. Something he had always taught us was that we must never ever be envious of the man/woman who seems to have it all (wealth, riches, huge house, etc.), because we don't know what he or she did to get it and also how they spend their time at nights, whether at rest or not.

Dr. Blair was a successful eye doctor. He came from very humble beginnings and he never ever forgot about that, nor did he ever let his success go to his head and treat his fellow man differently, as so many other doctors in this profession did. Yes, he made the prices of his services affordable to reach all classes of people. There were so many other doctors in this same field whom I found to be exploiting others and were in the business to "get rich soon" and so they did, or so it seemed. However, I saw and learned how Dr. Blair's kindness did not only extend to his immediate family, but also to all the people and their families that he serviced. His business was on a small scale, because it was he who alone prepared all the glasses for his patients. That means that after testing each patient's eyes and prescribing them with glasses only if they really needed them, then he had to complete the rest of the work. On the other hand, some doctors were prescribing every single person (whom went into their office) with glasses even if they didn't need them. If the prescribed lenses were not already readily available, Dr. Blair had to grind down some very thick lenses to fit the person's prescription. Many years ago, he used to have somebody assist with that aspect of the job, but sometimes that person stole the lenses and sold them to other optometrists. Once the lenses had been ground down, then Dr. Blair had to cut and shape them to fit each frame and fix them in as accurately and as precisely as possible. Also, when the patients came to collect their glasses, he liked to be the one to place them on the patient's face and have them test it out before leaving the office. That was a lot of work for one person to do and it entails a lot of standing which eventually would lead to you developing back pains, or even pains in general, around different parts of your body.

A few things I have learnt is how to tighten the backs of the temples to fit more smugly around the patient's ears, or if it's too tight how to relax it so it doesn't continue to pinch them behind the ears. Also I know how to slightly curve the frame so the patient's eyes can adjust to the frame and its lenses. I also know how to put back in lenses if they have dropped out of a spectacle frame. I know that some patients' lenses are spherical while others are cylindrical and I can check people's glasses and tell which ones are. To me, all that has been interesting and maybe, just maybe, I could have studied to be a technician and then maybe I may have been able to better assist my uncle.

At times I was amazed by how my uncle, Dr. Blair had some light moments with his patients, just like he did with us at home. Dr. Blair loved to show us "magic" and one of the tricks was to extend his thumb from a clenched fist and that made it seem like he was actually stretching it or pulling it out and pushing it back in. Many times Dr. Blair would ask some of his patients what was the meaning of their names or their children's names (especially if it was of African origin). Many of them didn't know. They just used those names because they sounded great or pleasant, when in fact, many times their meanings were not so.

To do this job we had to be a people's person and wanted to serve others. We were and we all were also so patient with the patients. Sometimes some patients wanted to spend so much time deciding on a spectacle frame (although we had given them our best judgment and suggestions), and some weren't satisfied until they asked Dr. Blair's opinion afterwards. Of course Dr. Blair was busy trying to test other patients' eyes and at times there would be quite a few patients waiting to see him again (and this was not really necessary). So much patience went into this job that lots of people didn't know or didn't realize just how taxing it could be. But you had to show lots of understanding once you were working with people. I have enjoyed working with my uncle for the time that I did, because I was able to see how he conducted himself in his professional life and that has definitely helped me. As I performed my duties I felt that I was being of service to people and it was a good feeling.

I have met and interacted with quite a lot of people during the course of my working life there. Some of the young men that I have met while working there tried to be extra friendly with me so as to get them faster service, or preferential treatment, but that didn't work, because I knew what they were trying to do. However, there were at least two special young men who were clients of Dr. Blair and they showed an interest in me. I was attracted to both of them, oh yes I was. Nevertheless, over time I decided not to be with the younger, sexier looking guy, because I felt that his handsome looks would mean lots of other girls and stiff competition for me. However, I decided to choose Estwick Morris, the older and less handsome-looking young man (smile). So, after dating for a while we got married.

CHAPTER 6

My life during the years 1980 and 1982

I started working at the Nursery or Pre-K school in February 1980. The school was not far away from my home so getting to and from work was no problem, because the school was just in the next block and the next street from where I lived. I enjoyed working with those little children and it was at that time when I realized just how much influence a teacher has on a child.

I learned a great deal from those students as well as my colleagues. And the more I did it, the better I felt about making that choice to become a teacher. I continued working at that Nursery school up to the end of the school year in July 1980. When I got married I was no longer working for Dr. Blair, but working for the government in the Education Ministry as a Nursery School teacher. It was always my dream to become a teacher when I got older, so I had started to fulfill my dream. I guess it was in my blood to become an educator since my dad too was an educator. I was subsequently admitted to the Cyril Potter College of Education, one of our colleges that teaches and trains you to become a teacher. The colleges and our university all work according to the same three terms as in the school system, and we begin in September – December, then January – April, then late April – early July. I had a few months to prepare for my start date in September, but my baby boy, Mervyn S. Morris was also due and was born on September 3, 1980, 1 day after Estwick's (my husband) birthday. Oh it was a joy to set eyes on this tiny little being and just see now how he has grown up to be so big, tall and handsome.

During the middle of September, 1980 I started attending the teachers' training college. It was a two year program where we were exposed to an academic program as well as hands-on teaching experiences. Most of the first year was academics with a few visits to different schools to observe classroom teachers. Later, we went out as a team to schools, where each one of us had to teach an individual subject while the others observed. Afterwards, we sat and discussed all the positives and negatives and when we returned to the college, we planned how we would fix all the negatives. To me that first year went by so quickly. Then it was time to look forward to the second year when we would be the seniors in college. That second and final year was a lot different from the first, because we had more teaching practice. Some days we were teaching for half a day or at times the entire day. We also had to do some community work, individual study and serve for a period of time in the National Service (one of our country's armed forces at that time). I enjoyed the time I spent in our teachers' training college because it prepared me for what I had to do once I had graduated as a first class trained teacher.

Picture of Mervyn and me in September 1981

During December of 1981, Lionel Malcolm Charles had returned to Guyana to marry my sister Leslyn Olivia Wilson. They had a beautiful wedding on January 2, 1982 and of course my uncle was the one to walk Leslyn down the aisle, then to give her hand in marriage to Malcolm. We enjoyed ourselves as we had worked so hard. I remember my mom reflecting after the wedding that "nobody else better don't get married around Christmas time", because we had to prepare for Christmas and then for the wedding coming right behind that. We really were very tired as we had done so much of the work, but it was well worth it as we have a wonderful brother-in-law who is really very much like our brother and mom's son, and not son-in-law.

Picture of Leslyn & Malcolm's wedding in January 1982

Chapter 7

My first schools as a first class trained teacher

The first school that I worked at after graduating in June 1982 was Russdale Primary which was located on Barr Street in Kitty. Since I was "infant trained", my appointment was to a Preparatory A or Kindergarten classroom. Of course I loved being in this grade as so many of the students came to school with no prior schooling and when they left after spending a year with me, we all could see how much they had learnt. At this school I met Enid Duff-King and other wonderful teachers whom I became close to. At that time Enid was teaching another Preparatory A and she was a great mentor to me for that first year, and our families became very close as well. At the end of that school year in July 1983, Russdale Primary was turned into a secondary school, so we had to be moved over to a new school they had just built in David Street Kitty.

F. E. Pollard Primary was opened in September of 1983 and it combined two schools from right in the neighborhood. It was a larger school and brand new, but I can remember that they were about to open and didn't even have all the furniture for the classrooms. Now that was very interesting, where would these students sit and do their work? Hhmm, We all thought. I remember when the parents brought their children to school and saw no furniture in my room, they asked where their child would sit. I apologized and said with a very sad face that for today they would have to sit on the floor as the furniture had not yet arrived.

The parents were annoyed, who wouldn't be especially with the new school uniforms (in Guyana all schools wore uniforms) that the children were wearing. However, reluctantly, the parents allowed their children to sit on the floor and we were able to start school on time that day. I worked at F.E. Pollard from September 1983 up to May 1989. It was wonderful working along there with the various staff members, and eventually meeting one of my own relatives there. This female relative was related to my mother's side of the family and we had worked together for about four years before we knew that we were relatives. In fact, it was only in February 1988 when my uncle Dr. Blair passed that Clarissa Ashe, my relative, came to school and told me that we were related. Her mom was one of the Kendall sisters who were related to my mom and uncle. Clarissa has always been a very quiet, patient, loving and caring person. Although she has migrated to the United States of America as well as myself, we still try to keep the lines of communication open.

Some of the other wonderful persons I have met at F.E. Pollard Primary are Clarissa Hall-Paul, Dianne Henry and Brenda Hardy-Ottley. We have made a great connection and still plan to someday hold a reunion to "catch up" with each other. I was still working at this school, when our lone university, University of Guyana (UG), began its first part-time classes offering studies in Bachelors' Degrees as well as Diploma Certificates. The programs were to begin in September 1987 and to be conducted over a five-year period, for the Bachelors', and a three- year period, for the Diplomas, with the classes being offered in the afternoons starting at 4:00 p.m. daily for five days. I was intrigued by this, because I had always wanted to further my education. I saw this as my opportunity to get ahead with my studies, so I quickly applied to complete my Bachelor's degree in Management, as I was preparing myself to get into the corporate world, or at least moving on up to teaching at a higher level (Business in the Secondary/High Schools).

It was tough going to classes after working all day and still having to go home and look after a family. But this is what both Estwick and I signed up for, so we both can complete our tertiary level education. As time went by, I continued with my classes, studies, assignments and exams. In some areas, I really had to work harder to maintain my grades, but I was committed to being successful and completing my program in the specified time.

Sometime during my second year at the university, my head teacher or principal had me teach our third standard or grade four and I was not too willing to move from the kindergarten class (the class I could teach with my eyes closed) all the way up to the grade four. It wasn't that I doubted my capabilities, but that it was not in my best interest in regards to my studies. I would now have to take my "out-of-school time" and prepare the content matter for my new students. This is the time that I would need to do my personal studies. So I felt it was not fair for either my students or me. I really didn't want to do this during the school year, but I had to seek another job in order to continue to be successful with my studies.

I was reminded that before I left F. E. Pollard, I had praised and congratulated one of my students so much that it stuck in her head. Akila (Kim) Ashe (Clarissa Ashe's daughter), believed that she could set out to achieve anything that she put her mind to. And she surely did. She went onto two of the country's top senior high schools, then continued her education at the University of Guyana. I am glad that I have had such an impact on my students, because all I wanted to do was to help them explore and discover the world.

CHAPTER 8

Thomas Stoll, Dias & Company 1989 - 1990

In May of 1989, right after I had left the teaching profession, I started to work at one of our top privately-owned accounting firms. I had realized that book-keeping and accounting were very interesting subjects, so I decided to pursue this field for a while. This firm was owned and controlled by an East Indian descendant, as many of the private firms were, and many people of African descend were not employed there. I considered myself to be one of the fortunate ones to have been employed there. The building was a beautiful, well designed concrete structure and it was equipped with air conditioning. This was the second privately-owned business I was employed at, but this one was on a much larger scale than my uncle's.

After about 4 months of employment, one of the seniors recommended me for a promotion. I am a very modest person and was very nervous and doubted that I was capable of performing with the type of caliber that was expected. So, without even talking it over with other seniors, I declined the position. When other seniors heard that I had turned down a promotion, they were so upset with me. They said I should have taken the promotion first then worry about other things after. But that is not how I operate. Nevertheless, in about 2 months time, I was offered another promotion, and as the senior was speaking with me, she asked me if I was now ready to accept the promotion. Very confidently, I told her that I was definitely ready to accept the promotion now. No sooner than I had accepted the promotion, I was sent out on location with my team of 4 members.

What made this somewhat difficult for me was that 2 of my team members had joined the company before me and now here I was as their team leader. However, before the end of the day I knew that they held no biases against me and we definitely worked well together. After this job was successfully completed and as my thoughts raced back, I asked myself why on earth I didn't take that promotion the first time it was offered. I also remember meeting with one of the Senior partners of the company before my promotion and he had asked me if I was ready for the promotion this time. Of course I reassured him that I had obtained more experience and was only too willing to take on that added responsibility.

During June of 1989, Joan Sewlall returned to Guyana from the United States of America and got married to my cousin/brother Bernard. It was a very beautiful wedding and we all had a great time as we enjoyed the wedding. My mom and sister Leslyn did not make that trip back home (from the USA) and we really did miss them. At that time Lynella Allyson Charles, Leslyn's and Malcolm's daughter was just about 10 months old and mom was her live-in baby sitter. This was about 1 year and 4 months after my uncle had passed and he was gravely missed as he was not there to be with Bernard and the rest of us on this very auspicious occasion. However, I felt his presence there and I am sure others felt it too.

Picture of Bernard and Joan's
wedding on June 1989

I spent a year working at Thomas, Stoll, Dias & Company and apart from enjoying my time there, I learnt a great deal. During that same year, the company's name was changed to Deloitte & Touché as the partners had obtained some ownership in that company. Auditing work is different from accounting, but you must have a knowledge of accounting to be able to complete an auditing job. Something that I had liked about this job was that we were always going to different locations or job sites to complete our work. So, you were never at one location for two long a time and also our team members would change as well. Once the senior had a job to be completed, he/she would call for a group of persons to sit in a meeting and the senior would then give an outline of what the job entailed. The name of the client, the length of the job, or anything else of importance that the senior felt you needed to know was discussed at that point in time. Then most importantly, the senior named the team leader with whom he/she needed to have a one-on-one meeting immediately afterwards. So, while the senior was meeting with the team leader, the members would go to the office manager and request the previous year's files for that client. Once the team leader left that one-on-one briefing, he/she immediately went to the rest of the team and informed them of their individual assignments. Depending on a number of factors, the team could either go to location immediately, or stay in the office for a few more hours doing some research, then head out after lunch or meet at the client's place of business in the morning. The size of the client always determined how much time was spent on location as well as the number of members that would be required for the job. The length of time could be anywhere from as little as 3 days to as much as 3 weeks or more. There was no need to visit some clients if their organizations were very small, so, we would stay in the office and complete their audit there. Most, if not all of the clients that I have worked at were very friendly and courteous towards my team and me and they always made us feel as part of their team whenever we were on location.

I can remember my cousin/sister, Golda was also studying at the University at the same time as I was and she did her work study stint at our company. This was during the August/Summer break, as the Educational systems in Guyana, usually shut down at the end of our school year which was in early July. Golda and I were never on the same team, so we never worked together, but on a few occasions we would be in the office together for a while. It was customarily that the partners would hold a Christmas party for the staff every year at one of the partners' house. The best part of this was that we the employees, didn't have to contribute to this as the partners used their money to treat us. Everybody seemed different in the sense that we were not in a work environment and we more or less, let down our hair and had lots of fun. Each staff member also received a gift from the partners as well as a bonus. Apart from working with my uncle, this was the only private company I had been working at, so the party and the bonus were all a big surprise to me, and a welcome one indeed.

The New Year began and I continued working and studying. However, the end of my third year at UG was approaching and I realized that my studies were becoming more difficult. I needed more time to prepare for my studies and I was not doing as well as I would have liked. So, I began to seriously consider my options, as to how I could make my studies easier. I took into consideration my living expenses for myself and son if I decided to stop working and go to UG full-time. I had money saved in the bank that would cover my personal day-to-day expenses and with Estwick contributing to Mervyn's monthly expenses, we would be fine. Despite the fact that I enjoyed doing the auditing work, my final decision was to leave the job and then I would have the whole day and much more time to fully concentrate on my studies and perform much better. So, sadly, at the end of August, I resigned from my job with Deloitte and Touché.

CHAPTER 9

University of Guyana - Full Time 1990 - 1992

When UG opened again in September 1990, I was now unemployed and going to school full time so as to prepare for my studies. My program was still a part-time one with classes starting after 4:00 p.m. in the afternoons. This was indeed good for me, because now I had more time for my studies and I definitely took advantage of the free time and got to campus early in the mornings. At first I used to go to the library and sit there to do whatever research I had to do, or complete any assignments. But after a while, one of my friends convinced me to go to an unoccupied classroom and study. At least there we could utilize the chalkboard to help solve any problems, and we didn't have to speak in hushed tones. I found this to be very beneficial to me as the more time I spent on something the better I understood it as well as remembered it.

My study partner was a male and we were in the same program. So, generally, every day we were studying together. Many people saw us together all the time and didn't know the extent of our friendship, so they interpreted it how they wanted. When we realized that people thought we were in a relationship, we allowed them to think so and on a few occasions we even "over did it" by having some loud conversations so they could hear more. For instance, on one occasion I can distinctly remember us walking away from each other and he turned around and loudly said "I'm going to bring it tonight when I come". Of course anybody hearing that would be convinced that we were indeed in a relationship. We were playing and anybody who was our very close friend knew who his girlfriend was as she was right there on campus with us. One of the reasons my study mate and his girlfriend didn't really hang out together was that they were not in the same program as us, thus their free times were not the same. I can even remember one of our very close friends was trying to tell another person that I was not my study mate's girlfriend, but they would not believe her. So the word was going around campus that "Joe" (some people called him) had a girlfriend with a short "jerry-curl" hairstyle. I was the person wearing the "short jerry-curl" hairstyle, but I was not Joe's girlfriend, just his study mate and a real good friend as we both confided in each other.

During our times of studies, we have had so many different and interesting experiences that at times it made me smile when I remembered some of them. One such memory was what happened during our 1990 -1991 school year when Joe and I had a very difficult Law assignment. At first, it took us a lot of time to just correctly interpret the question (as so many others had different interpretations and thus different responses). However, we eventually narrowed down our various thoughts and ideas and put together a great answer, or what we thought to be a great answer. This was an individual assignment, and as we had worked together, Joe decided to change a few words and phrases just so it wouldn't appear that we had copied. We turned in our assignments to our professor and after about 2 weeks, the assignments were returned. This professor was our Chief Justice (we only had one for our entire country) and as such his standards were extremely high, so when Joe received his paper, he was so elated with his B grade. But his glee was short lived when he saw my grade. The professor had given me an A grade. WOW! I felt so happy when I had first received my grade, but then a bit surprised and disappointed after seeing my friend's grade knowing all the hard work that we had put in. Joe was upset and couldn't understand the difference in the marking, but he dared not ask Justice B. about it. We had worked together, however, nothing said that we couldn't work together. Joe took our papers around the class and asked our classmates to read both of them and then explain the differences in them that would warrant a different grade. Nobody could identify the differences, and Joe just shrugged it off and left it at that. Later he could have gone to the professor and asked for his recommendations to help him improve his paper for the future. I knew he was upset and I was very disappointed. Nevertheless, Joe very quickly put that incident out of his mind and focused on what lay ahead for him.

As I look back at my fourth year at U.G. 1990 -1991 and the first time attending as a full time student, I see how that was my best decision indeed. I was able to concentrate more on my studies and my grades were definitely much better. Also, I liked being a full time student. I have no regrets, but I look back at that time and see that I should have made more time for my son, Mervyn, as during that same period, he had entered into the fourth standard class (grade 5). Now remember this was a very important time for our students in Guyana, because in this class, we sat our SSEE or Secondary School Entrance Examination. The senior secondary schools were said to be the better of the two and students could attend them for either 5 or 7 years, depending on the students' choices. The junior secondary schools catered for students from Form 1 to Form 5, or Grade 6 to grade 10, while the senior secondary schools catered for students from Form 1 to Form 6 or grade 6 to grade 12.

Mervyn had passed his exams in April of 1991 and that earned him a place at Bishops' High School, a former all-girls school, one of the top senior secondary schools. His aunt Neibert, former Bishops' High student was very instrumental with assisting him with his homework. I know he learned good study habits from being around me and by also observing how I studied. Estwick was a bit disappointed, although he had no real impact on Mervyn's studies. He had hoped that Mervyn would have passed for Queens' College, another top senior secondary school, and also a former all boys school. But Mervyn was happy, and we were so very proud of him. We knew all the hard work that he had put in and he had indeed earned it.

My last year at U.G. was my best year, because by then I had got into a routine and it was functioning well. I worked the hardest and my results paid off. I was so proud of myself. For some reason the classes didn't seem as difficult to manage as my earlier years, but this could have been that I got smarter or was just coping with things much better. In the latter part of May in 1992, Golda, my cousin/sister and I graduated from the University of Guyana with our Bachelors' degrees. Hers was in Accountancy and mine was in Management. Our families were in full attendance at our graduation ceremony and Golda and I were just following the lead of our older siblings and completing our bachelors at U.G. I can vividly remember us taking pictures and in one of them, Mervyn was just leaning down on Auntie Beryl's shoulder, because he was taller than her.

From left to right, me, Joey, Mervyn, aunty (in rear) aunty Beryl (in front), Neibert,
Golda and Wain, Golda's friend (That's all I knew at this time.)

CHAPTER 10

Guyana National Engineering Corporation & Inland Revenue Department 1992 - 1995

It was so nice to finally be finished with my studies and now get some more time to rest and socialize with friends and family. However, after graduating it was time to get on with life and begin some job searching. The first place that I started to work at was Guyana National Engineering Corporation (GNEC) in Lombard Street, Georgetown. I was offered the position of Manager Trainee and I had 3 persons who would report to me. Most of the work was Accounts and I was scared. That previous feelings of inadequacy and failure re-entered my head and I felt too ashamed to even go to talk to my supervisor about some of my doubts. I knew later that part of it was now having new responsibilities and having also others depending on me. I went to work for that entire week feeling nervous and really guilty, because of what I was planning to do. I took the coward's way out and decided not to return to that job for the second week. So, I got my son involved and sent him to my manager on Monday morning with a letter informing him that I wouldn't be returning to work. I can't remember what happened after that, but I try not to think about it, since whenever I look back, I see that as one of my failures.

However, it was in January 1993 that I was again offered employment. This time it was at IRD or Inland Revenue Department another government facility. I really don't know what it was about that job that I decided to take it and didn't feel that I would have had a difficult time with it. It could be that in this job, I was not put into a supervisory role, but was working along with other clerks as we examined the income taxes that were submitted by various companies. Also, when I started to work with IRD, there were 2 other recent graduates from my class whom I had already known.

The job consisted of some auditing as well as accounting. We would go through the company's files to see what they had submitted for the income tax years and determine whether or not they had submitted the correct amount of taxes. We used their source documents as a reference just to account for all of their income. If we had other information that showed them receiving undeclared income, we would immediately get in contact with the company and request them to submit additional records. This process could take a long time, so we worked on more than 1 file at a time. Whenever we needed documentation from the client, we sent out our field officers who went directly to the client to obtain the requested documents. There was another recent graduate like myself, Elizabeth Lambert-Daly, but she worked in the Audit department. At times she told me about all the excitement she was experiencing as she was able to locate more taxes than what was originally declared by the individuals. As I continued to work there, I found that quite a few companies had understated their income.

After a little over one year, I was transferred to the Audit department which was right next door to the Companies department. This department was doing audits on individuals. Now my friend Liz and I got a chance to work closer together and compare the ways that some of these individuals tried to hide their income. There were some very interesting ways, but some of these people forgot that other people kept a paper trail and that was such an easy way to find money, once we cross-referenced. For instance Liz had a client's notebook where he recorded every penny that he gave to anybody, or loaned them as well as the dates. He was very good at keeping his records although it was not in the usual conventional way. As a result, IRD was able to use such source documents to locate individuals' undisclosed income.

It was while working at IRD that I learned to crotchet. I never ever thought about it before, I just always admired all the beautiful crotchet items that I saw. During our hour-long lunch break, Liz used to crotchet various items either for her own home or for sale. Sometimes I would sit and talk to her as she was doing so. I also noted that she was a very quick worker and sometimes, although she looked away, she still didn't miss a stitch. One day as I was admiring her, she asked me if I wanted to learn. I felt it was too difficult and said not really. But she convinced me that it was really very simple, because there weren't that many stitches to learn.

So, she advised me as to the type of beginner's needle I needed to purchase as well as the type of thread to use. So, the very next day, I purchased my tools and she started off by teaching me the very basic chain stitch. Oh yes, it was very simple but how to use the chains was the tricky step. At the beginning I was looking very clumsy and holding the needle and thread in an awkward position. Then as days went by, my positioning got much better. It all had to do with practicing and the frequency of it. Not long after I was making "chair-backs" (decorations to hang over the top of the sofas), center-pieces for the coffee tables, cushions, table cloths and eventually even women's tops.

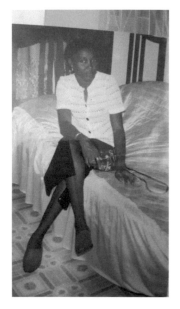

Picture of me with a crotchet
top that I had made

I was enjoying this new experience and I kept challenging myself to go ahead and make any other decorations that looked appealing to me. I can also remember making a zodiac sign and then framing it and presenting it to one of my friends on his birthday. He was pleasantly surprised and was also surprised that I knew how to crotchet and also that I found the time to do so.

Working at IRD had caused me to start filing my taxes, as I was a delinquent citizen, and how can I go after someone when I myself was not setting the example. It caused me to really see the significance and benefits of paying my taxes. I have learned a lot from working at Inland Revenue Department, and I had also met quite a few very friendly persons both employees and clients. However, promotion there was not easily forth-coming as there were so many persons on the same level that it would take years for that to happen. So, after spending a few years there, it was time to move on.

Two years after Golda's graduation from UG, the "mystery Wain" got married to Golda on July 23, 1994. I say "mystery Wain", but not in a bad way. It was just that at our graduation I was just introduced to Wain as her friend, not her 'boyfriend'. Yes, Enoch Wain Gaskin got the stamp of approval from us and so he and Golda got married. It was the first wedding that I had attended with full military honors and that along with the entire bridal party made it a fantastic wedding. By then Bernard, my cousin/brother was living in the United States of America and he had returned for this beautiful occasion. Malcolm, Leslyn, Lynella (she was the beautiful flower girl) and mom had also returned for the wedding. It was a picturesque event and we enjoyed it greatly.

Golda and Wain's wedding in July 1994

CHAPTER 11

Demerara Distilleries Limited 1995 - 1996

I started to work at Demerara Distilleries Limited (DDL) in June of 1995. I had applied for a position that was advertised at their headquarters in downtown Georgetown. However, when they employed me, they stationed me out of town at a village called Diamond on the East Bank of Demerara. This village is located at 6.75 miles or 10.86 kilometers from Georgetown. Diamond was one of the many distilleries owned and operated by DDL. At these distilleries, the workers use sugar and other ingredients to make soda and alcoholic beverages like rum. In the laboratory, the chemist does the mixing and the distillery manager has the final say about the products, before they were released for final approval from the head-office.

A number of departments at the distillery were indirectly involved in the successful production of the rum. I was employed as the Manager trainee and despite my work was mainly in the office, I too would walk around the distilleries meeting and greeting employees as I observed them performing their various jobs. Some of my responsibilities were handling the Petty Cash, completing weekly and monthly reports as well as incident reports and most importantly finalizing the pay sheets and paying the employees. There were both weekly paid as well as monthly employees. A few times the weekly employees' wages were not calculated correctly by their supervisors and I might not have caught it before inputting the payroll. You can imagine how they felt when on Friday after opening their pay envelopes they found that their money was short. What was so interesting to note, is that a number of these weekly workers did not know how to read or write well, but they definitely knew when their money was short and they did not behave nicely. However, whenever that happened, I could solve that problem in different ways. I usually spoke with and apologized to the employee(s), then depending on the amount that was short, I might be able to pay them with the balance of my petty cash. Or I would just have to add their payment for that week to the upcoming week. Of course this was difficult for the employees and I would definitely feel bad about this, because it could mean that I was not doing my job properly in rechecking after the supervisors had computed their sectional payroll.

However, I would have a meeting with the different supervisors of the departments to try to ensure that they took more responsibilities when performing their duties. Also, my immediate supervisor, the manager of the entire distillery, also told them that if they kept making these mistakes so often, then he would authorize me to use part of their paycheck to pay these unfortunate employees. Now we knew that the manager was trying to show them how serious he was and didn't really literally mean that. But we also knew that if this manager got real tired of the frequent mistakes, he definitely could carry out his threat. Nevertheless, we never had to implement that as we all tried our very best to get it right the first time. Most of the times we got it correct.

There was an incident when one of our "laborers" got hurt whilst doing his job. He had cut his hand, so it was the employers' responsibility to take him for medical treatment. The injured worker, the chemist and I got in the car with our driver and we made our way down to the hospital in Georgetown. We spent a very long time at the hospital with the worker, and when he was finally seen, we put him in a public mini-bus to return home. This vehicle operated like a taxi but picked up a bus load of 9, 10 or 11 people depending on its size. Our driver had long gone home as he had to return the car at the end of his work day. This distillery was a very safe place to work and we never had to take another employee to the hospital whilst I was there for that year. In fact, there were strict safety rules that all employees had to adhere to every day.

During the rest of my stay there, everything went fine, there were no exciting things happening. Every day the distillery was open and working as they had to keep on producing, but my work days were only from Mondays to Fridays. At the end of my first year with the distillery, I left as the traveling to and from work was getting to me. It was not a far journey, but I wasn't accustomed to traveling out of Georgetown to go to work. I did not own a car as they were very expensive and I had to depend on public transportation, such as mini busses, to take me to and from work. On my way to work in the mornings, I had to walk out to the main road and catch a bus to go down-town. Then at the bus park I would board another bus to take me to my location. Then on my return home, I did the same thing, but they were so many people on the road and it was a great big jostle and maybe a fight to get on a bus.

I felt it was time to move on to another job and of course, I began to miss my August vacations off, as well as being in the classroom. So, I started researching private schools as they were better paid than the Government schools. My cousin/sister informed me of a new school that was about to open for the new school year 1996 – 1997. So, I called the number and set up an appointment time to meet with the owners and administrators.

During Easter/Spring of 1996, we had gone on a 1 week vacation to Barbados and we met some of our cousins, also vacationing in Barbados at that time. Neibert, Mervyn and I had traveled from Guyana, while Malcolm, Leslyn, Lynella and mommy had traveled from the USA. Our cousin Sister Pansy was in Barbados vacationing with her 2 grandchildren, Whitney and Wilet (Petal's children).

Picture of Whitney, Lynella and Wilet in Barbados 1996

CHAPTER 12

Private School - SON August 1996 - August 2000

The meeting went well with the owners and administrators of the private school. They had already got permission from the Guyana government to open their school and they named it SON as it represented people from all different nations of the world. The two owners, a husband and wife couple, were British born and the administrator was American born. They were all Caucasians and moving to a South American country where the majority population was definitely not Caucasians or Europeans. However, I believe that some type of a feasibility study was done before they decided to embark on this plan. It was known that at that time, Guyana did not have many privately owned schools and both the students and staff would definitely benefit from this type of Educational facility.

In a few short weeks after my interview, I received a telephone call informing me that I was offered a teaching job at the SON when it opened in September of 1996. A hard copy came in the mail later. My position was a primary 2, or grade 3 class teacher. Of course I was very elated to hear this, but also anxious to hear about the next steps. We, the teachers who were offered a one year contract, had to collaborate and create a curriculum for the school. This was the first time that I had ever signed a contract. This school was to cater for students from ages 3 years to 14 years old adding on a class or grade every year, until they reached the final level of high/secondary school. So, when the school began it catered for Nursery/Pre-K up to Primary 4 or Grade 5 in the Primary/Elementary department and from Form 1 or Grade 6 to Form 3 or Grade 8 in the Secondary/High school department. Now, I had been out of the classroom for a number of years, so the other primary teachers were able to obtain copies of the government issued curriculum from the Nursery class all the way up to primary 4. When we sat down with the Administrators and owners, we discussed some pertinent aspects of the curriculum as they were about to combine their ideas with what we had from the government. It took us a little over a week to compile the

A picture of my Primary 2/Grade 3 students
and myself at our December party in 1996

curriculum for the school year and then we examined the building and began to prepare our classrooms.

When school started in September 1996, we had a very small number of students enrolled from Nursery all the way up to form 3. We only had one class of each level and I can't remember the total number of children we had attending, but I started out with 11 students in my class. It was a good experience teaching this smaller class size, because there were so many activities that I did with the students. One thing that struck me that was different in the private schools was that we only had one register per class for both boys and girls. Whilst in the public school, we had two registers, one for the girls and the other for the boys. Also, in the private school after we did the attendance, we submitted that to the office for them to keep a record of that. But, in the public schools, after we submitted our attendance daily to the office, we had to do a weekly count of our attendance, then monthly, termly and finally yearly. At the end of the public school year we had to balance our registers and it was not always easy to do. Many times there were small challenges and the numbers wouldn't always balance immediately.

However, as the school year progressed, more students enrolled and we had a very successful first year. At the end of the school year, a new 1 year contract was signed again by the teachers who were returning for the new school year.

The 1997-1998 school year started with us having the school building extended since we now had more students and were up to two classes per grade level, while the secondary department had added another form and that took them up to form 4 or grade 9. This brought a new promotion for me in the form of a lead teacher position. I was in charge of the primary 1 or grade 2 and primary 2 or grade 3 classes, so I had to hold regular meetings with those teachers and we discussed any problems, students or otherwise. Later, on a bi-weekly basis, all the lead teachers would meet with the administrator to keep her informed of our issues and problems as well as our suggestions. We attended faculty meetings once a month, and only if there was an urgency, then we would have to attend another meeting during the month. A swimming pool was added this New Year too. I had only just learned how to swim a few years before, so I was excited to get as many opportunities as possible to practice. Swimming was scheduled on one of the students P.E. classes every week, and it was a requirement that the class teacher accompany his/her class to assist the P.E. teacher with managing the students in the pool. It was such fun as most of the students already knew how to swim and the others were eager to learn. So, every week my students and I looked forward to our swim day when we would get a great opportunity to relax a bit as we practiced different swim techniques in the pool.

During this school year, the students also began to learn Spanish and French. In our public schools at that time, foreign languages were not learnt at the primary level, but at the secondary. So, the children attending were definitely at an advantage as compared to the students in the public school setting. We were able to take our students out on more field trips as we had acquired a bus which was able to accommodate at least 2 classes at a time, remember we had small class sizes. As we made full use of the bus and all those trips, we were definitely enriching our curriculum, making it hands-on as well as exciting and interesting. These are some of the things that made learning fun for the students and kept them engaged.

Also during this year, the administrator decided to increase my salary as I was the only primary teacher who had a first degree (this was not a requirement for the position). Of course, some of the employees were made aware of my increase (not through me) and were upset about it, because as they said, my degree was not within the field of education. But as I informed one of the disgruntled staff members, I never stopped them from furthering their education and I couldn't see why I should not be compensated for my extra time studying. However, that was the end of the matter, or at least for me, and I didn't hear anything about it later.

As time went by, our school got more involved in activities that were sponsored by the government. Many of those activities were in the Sporting department. From the school's inception, we had our own inter house sports competition. These were usually competition among each other right there in the school and it was mainly in the form of races/sprints and later it involved other games. At our annual inter house sports we would also have the teachers' races and I used to participate in the female's 100 meters race and win it every year, with stiff competition coming from the primary 3 or grade 4 teacher.

One Easter Monday, the Porters family invited Neibert and me to spend it with them at a creek. So, we used a car and a mini bus to transport us all to and from the creek. We totally enjoyed our outing

Pictures of Easter Monday 1997 at the creek with some of the Porter generation

During our 1998 – 1999 school year, the school year began and we had a very good start as per usual. I noticed that at all the schools that I had taught, our students were always so well behaved and respected all staff or even adults' authority. I never had discipline problems, nor had the need to call in parents for their child's disruptive behavior. It just goes to show how well-mannered our students were and it didn't matter from which part of the country or the world they came, they had to get in line and follow the rules.

Christmas of 1998 was a very good one for both my personal family and school family. We enjoyed it to the fullest and as usual the time off from school was always so relaxing and refreshing. However, sadly on the night of December 31st, my oldest cousin/brother died as a result of an accident. As I mentioned previously, this day was my second oldest cousin's/brother's birthday as well as Old Year's night (big occasion for us). The sad part about this is that I didn't know anything about this until the next day, Friday January 1st, 1999.

Above is a picture of Peter sitting on his motorcycle/
motor scooter sometime before that fatal incident.

To this date, I really don't even know what happened, but I do know it was a very dark and rainy night and he was on his motorcycle/motor scooter. To see that he had overcome a very grave illness (Guillain-Barre syndrome – very rare condition where the immune system attacked the nerves and caused him paralysis) which started when he was 16 years old and had to be hospitalized for over a year. This struck our family a devastating blow and all the joys of seeing a new year seemed so dim now. However, because of our strong faith in God, he was able to wrap his arms tightly around us and bring us through it all. Thanks be to God! We may not understand it, nor do we know the reason why, or want to accept it, but at least all of these setbacks cause us to acknowledge our Lord God more, sing his praises and say "It's nothing but God!"

As the 1998 – 1999 school year progressed, we at SON, got involved in more government-run school activities. For instance, in February of 1999, we took part in our first ever Mashramani competition. From the beginning of the month of February there were lots of different types of competitions and celebrations leading up to the big Mashramani parade that was held on Republic Day February 23rd, later renamed Mashramani Day. The competitions were in the Fine Arts Department and included singing, dancing, poetry recitation, steel pan playing and even calypso singing. The competitions were divided into different age groups to allow participation from both the primary and secondary departments of the schools. Our P.E. and Art teachers decided that they wanted to have the school participate in the float parade. So, after it was discussed with the administrator and the owners, the decision was confirmed that SON will take part in its first-ever school wide competition. So, the gentlemen decided on how they would like us to depict the theme "Guyana in the New

Millennium" and after seeing their sketch as they explained their vision, we, the ladies decided how we were going to assist them with this big project.

We came up with a plan as to what we wanted to portray and then notified our students and parents via our administrator. As the time went by we began preparing the children's costumes and practicing their dances. We had asked for volunteers from the children and also informed them that we would be participating in the parade on February 23 rd. The children had become excited and so too did the teachers. Three days a week after school, we stayed back and practiced with the students. While we continued working with the students the artist and P.E. teacher continued to design their project. We continued working regularly with the students as we helped them get ready for their performance in February. Finally it was the day before the children's competition and we had not completed all the costumes nor was the float finished. We realized that this day was going to be a very late one, but we never anticipated it being an all- night affair. So, after we had completed the students' final practice, we sat down to complete all the costume pieces. One teacher was busily on the sewing machine, while the others were either trying to fix the props or adjusting materials on the main float. During the long night, we drank coffee, played music, sang songs and even got up and danced around to help keep us awake so we could complete the costumes.

Pictures of us working on our float

Each of us had a member of our immediate family bring us a fresh change of clothing and early in the morning before the students started to come to school, we went upstairs into the building, took our showers and prepared for school for that day. During the morning session of the school day, the P.E. teacher, one of the administrators and 4 of our students went off to the competition.

It was a highly competitive competition and our school was placed second. Our teacher representative was gravely upset as he said we followed their guidelines, worked way too hard and our costumes and float looked very impressive and were a very good representation of the theme (as many of the onlookers also said). However, SON finally accepted the second place prize as we didn't want to discourage our students who seemed somewhat confused and couldn't understand how we didn't win the first place.

It was later rumored that the judges believed that we had used imported materials on our float, so we were not awarded the first place prize. However, all the materials we used were local and nothing was imported.

Nevertheless, we tried to keep our students' spirits motivated so that they would attend the float parade in a few days-time. So on February 23rd bright and early, both staff and students who were participating assembled at the school's compound in preparation for the float parade. At the appointed time we left school and assembled at the starting point where we paraded throughout the streets of Georgetown along the parade route. We continued parading and dancing through the streets until we arrived at the National Park a few hours after we had begun. We had to dance around the park 2 times for the judges to have a good look at us and to be able to judge our performance. This was the first time that I had participated in a float parade and I enjoyed it tremendously. When the announcements were later made, we did not win the float parade, but after what had happened earlier, we weren't surprised and just didn't allow that to steal our joy. We were just glad that the students enjoyed themselves as we the staff did too.

A picture of the students during the float parade

We came to the end of that school year and again it was another successful school year. By this time we had added forms right up to the fifth form or grade 10 and this is normally our exam forms in Guyana. So, we had students sitting for and writing their CXC, Caribbean Examination Council examinations in various subjects. Also, because we were affiliated with England, our students were also writing the GCE, General Council of Education examinations too. These examinations were done in England, countries that had a common interest in this exam as well as countries and islands in the Caribbean that were once under the British rule. When these results came back, our students had performed well, especially when you consider that this was the first time that students from our school had taken these exams. It just showed the good caliber of students we had as well as the dedication of our highly qualified teachers.

We continued on at SON adding students as time went by. During the 1999 – 2000 school year I went through a tough time when both my aunty Beryl and one of my close friends took ill. My friend Dee was suffering from a thermal disease and had sought treatment in England. However, it was too late for them to attend to her as it had already spread too far. So, she returned to Guyana and followed up with her doctor there. My aunty Beryl had been a hypertensive patient for many, many years. Unfortunately sometime in late February of 2000, she was home alone and suffered a stroke. We didn't know immediately, until later in the day when my sister and I returned home from work and found her besides her front door. We took her to the hospital where the doctor attended to her and then sent her home. The next day we took her to another doctor and hospital as her condition was not improving. Subsequently, she was admitted.

I began to visit my aunt twice a day as the hospital was very close to my school. Later, my friend Dee was also admitted to that same hospital. I visited my aunt twice a day and my friend once a day. My aunt had slipped into a coma by now and my friend was in constant pain, some days more so than

A picture of my aunt Beryl

others. However, I continued visiting them both for a couple of weeks, until very early on the morn of March 4th, I got the sad news that my friend had passed that morning. It was so sad that she didn't even live to reach her 40th birthday, which would have been celebrated on March 30th. Also, my aunt never came out of that coma and sadly on March 26th, she too passed. My mom and Leslyn flew to Guyana from the United States of America for my aunt's home going service. Mom stayed on for some months while Leslyn went back to the United States after about a week. Later, Neibert was the chaperone for both my mom and my aunt as she accompanied them to the USA. My mom was returning, while my aunt and Neibert were going for a holiday.

At our International airport as aunty and mom were leaving for the USA. Neibert was accompanying them as Golda, Mervyn, myself, Miriam and Ethan look on.

Chapter 13

August 2000 - December 16, 2000

Then came the 2000 – 2001 school year. This year started out just like any other and there was nothing out of the ordinary. However, during the month of October, I had an appointment date at the American Embassy in Georgetown, Guyana. My mother had sponsored my sister, Neibert, my son, Mervyn and I to come and live with her in the United States of America. So, we all went into the embassy (we all had the same date and time) on October 10, 2000 to meet with an American consular. After interviewing us for a little while, we were told to return that afternoon. Based on the procedure, we already knew that we would be granted the visas to travel. So, we left and got some lunch then returned promptly at 2:00 p.m. as per request. Shortly after we returned we were called into one of their rooms, congratulated and given the visas.

We were very happy to be granted these visas. It meant so much to all of us in different ways. However, one of the main things was that we would get to be with our mother again and now also my older sister, Leslyn and her family. Economics was also one of the other reasons for migrating. When we left the embassy, we went to Bel Air Park to first notify our aunt. She knew that our mom had filed the paperwork for us to go, but didn't know our status at that time. We informed her and our two cousins, Joey and Golda, who were all happy for us, but we know they would be sad to see us go. We have been so close all our lives.

Next, we went to those special cousins (the Porters) in Queenstown to inform them that we had just received our visas. We knew they were all happy for us, but that they too would also miss us greatly. When we returned home, we had to start making some decisions. The embassy gave us 6 months in which to leave the country. Now, when you are packing up your life and moving onto another country to start life all over again, it's not too easy to do. But we already knew that's what we were expected to do, so, we had to quickly figure out exactly what we were going to do with the contents of the house. The upcoming year 2001, was going to be Guyana's national elections and we felt there was going to be some type of unrest. As a result of this, we decided to leave the country in December before the year ended. This only gave us approximately 2 months in which to empty the house and leave, but we were determined to do so. We had never intended to sell the things in the house, but to give them away to relatives and close friends. So, over the next two months we started to give away all the things that we didn't plan to take with us. We made sure we booked our flight and secured that flight date of December 16, 2000.

Pictures of us on a Bartica trip in 2000

Golda planned a boat trip for us to a resort in Bartica. I had never been there before and had always heard so much about Bartica, so of course I was excited. It was a 1 day trip, so there was no cause to overnight. I enjoyed visiting some of the monuments there and also the waterfalls. On that trip too we were able to play games like table tennis, badminton, and cricket. Then of course we had to take a swim in the creek. I had previously learned how to swim, so now I was more comfortable being in the water.

We had planned to visit as many of our closest relatives and friends as we could and notify them that we were leaving. So, many afternoons after work, we paid them a visit and informed them of our travel date.

For a while though, we could not go and pay anybody a visit because I got sick over a weekend. This was strange as we had ordered some food from a Chinese cook shop and sometime after eating it I began throwing up. However, we thought it was food poisoning although I was the only one affected and don't know why we were thinking so. After that I couldn't keep anything down in my stomach, so Neibert and Mervyn took me to the doctor. He did his examinations and ran a bunch of tests, but the results of that showed nothing. I can remember him giving me some tablets, but even those didn't help me. I stayed away from school for a while but to no avail, nothing was working, my tummy was hurting and I just couldn't eat anything because it all came right back up. Most of the times the liquid diet worked, but at other times, absolutely nothing worked. As I wasn't eating much, I began to lose some weight, but never realized just how much it was until a friend saw me at Andrea Stephens' mom's funeral and commented about how much weight I had lost. He too had lost a lot of weight and I also commented about that to him.

I don't know for how long this continued, but sometime later I began to feel better, but I was still being careful with what I ate. I considered it a mystery illness because it was gone just as mysteriously as it came. Later, something happened to me that I had never experienced before and it was God talking to me. This only happened after I had got over this bout of sickness. I never realized the connection at that point in time, but after many years I realized that there was a connection. I cannot remember exactly when this happened, but as I was lying in bed very early one morning I heard God talking to me. So I began talking back to him and thanking him for all that he had done for me so far over all these years. I asked him to continue to keep watch over my family and to take us safely to this new land in USA and to always be watchful over us. This talking back turned into a prayer and I remember going at it for over an hour, but all the time I could feel like God was right there next to me holding me in his arms and comforting and reassuring me that all things would be well with my family.

My prayers and thanks to God appeared as if I were crying, but they were cries of joy. At first Neibert heard me and came over to my room to see if I was okay. So, once I reassured her, she returned to her room and subsequently her bed. A little while after that Mervyn too came over to check on me, so, I told him that I was fine and grateful to God. Obviously my sobs were loud and disturbed them both. I don't believe they were truly convinced that I was okay, because they had never ever seen me like that. But to me too that was different, as this was my first experience of talking with God and it was really interesting for me to hear him so clearly and know it was him.

Nevertheless, once I had started to feel better, we continued to visit the rest of our relatives and friends to inform them of our travel date. December 15, 2000 was the last day for school until after the Christmas break. So, this was our last day in Guyana, as we were traveling on Saturday morning, the next day to the USA. My students were so upset that I was leaving that they didn't even want to let me go. A couple of them literally held onto my leg at the end of the day and didn't want to release it. I had to tell them that I had something important to do before it was too late. I also had to take some time to sit down and talk with one of my former student's brother. He was of the impression that I didn't like him, because he said that I had taught his sister and wasn't going to be there to teach him. He was really serious and very upset, so I had to spend the time to try to make him understand the reason for me leaving at this point in time.

When I finally got home later that day, I had to finish packing my suitcases and tidy the house. Of course, I didn't sleep as well as I should have, but it must have been the excitement of the next day. The next morning came and we were off to the airport. I can remember having mixed feelings. Happy to be going to somewhere new, but also sad to be leaving the country and home I knew all my life. As we finally sat down in the airplane all buckled up and leaving our native land to take up residence in a foreign land miles and miles away, all I could remember was thinking about how I was going to start my life over in a New Land!

Printed in the United States
By Bookmasters